Dear Mister Ward

Complaint Letters to Montgomery Ward
from the American Heartland
1932-1942

Preserved and transcribed by
by Verna Sylvia Gregg

Edited and Annotated By
Evan Hopestill Gregg

For more information and merchandise based on the letters

Please visit

www.dearmisterward.com

Dedication

To my grandma for having the foresight to save these letters.

To my grandpa for buying the binder.

To my mom for teaching me to recognize a good story.

And to my dad for never throwing anything away.

I miss you all.

Introduction

Before there was Yelp, Facebook or Twitter there were formal complaints departments. Teams of people would process letters and telegrams from customers with gripes of all sizes and levels of weirdness. This was especially true for the pioneering mail order company Montgomery Ward, known for its policy of "Satisfaction Guaranteed or Your Money Back."

The letters in this book were saved by my grandma, Verna Gregg when she worked in the complaints department of the Montgomery Ward office in St Paul, Minnesota between 1932-1942.

Verna began working at Montgomery Ward after graduating from high school in 1932 and worked her way up to the role of correspondent. In that role she was responsible for composing responses to letters sent in by customers from all over the rural Midwest.

She was specifically in charge of complaint letters but she also translated letters from Swedish, Norwegian and German. She spoke her original responses to the letters into an Edison dictaphone that recorded on wax cylinders. The cylinders were then sent to a team of typists who would type the letter and send it in to her supervisor for approval.

Some of these letters stood out to her as especially amusing or touching, so she saved them. For many years she kept them loose in a box until one day my grandpa brought home a black binder with her name engraved on it. She then typed up the letters, painstakingly recreating many if not all of the typos and misspelled words, and put them in the binder.

When my grandpa died in 1981 my uncle uncovered the binder while clearing out the family home in Minonk, Illinois. The binder ended up with my father and when he passed away in 2018 I discovered it yet again while going through boxes.

I connected with the letters on a new level during the Covid-19 lockdown. They came from a place of isolation and unease that echoed the current situation. After I shared some of the letters online, friends who had seen them convinced me that they needed to be published.

These letters were sent in to Montgomery Ward by customers during the Great Depression and the early days of World War II. While many of their complaints may seem archaic and funny to us now, there is a timelessness to much of what they wrote. Some of these "letters" are just brief notes, but some are quite detailed. Although they were sent to the complaints department they aren't for the most part filled with vitriol or anger. Some are intentionally funny and may or may not be tongue-in-cheek. Many of them reflect an earnest desire on the customer's part to connect with a company that had had such an indelible impact on their lives.

When Montgomery Ward began in 1872 it was a lifeline for rural people and at times their only connection to the rest of civilization. While much had changed by the time these letters were written, they make clear the continued limitations of a rural existence.

There are many themes that repeat throughout the letters, and they could have been grouped in many different ways. I've organized them in a way that I hope tells a larger story about Montgomery Ward and the role it played in these customers' lives.

A Very Brief History
of Montgomery Ward

Montgomery Ward was started by Aaron Montgomery Ward in 1872. It started as a very small operation run by Mr. Ward and two partners as a side job. Mr Ward had a vision of a general catalog marketed directly at farmers. He started by using direct sales letters and pamphlets to reach farmers through their local agricultural groups known as Granges. His catalog soon grew in popularity and page count and within three years it featured 3,899 items over 152 pages.

While this was the first general catalog specifically for farmers, it was not the beginning of mail order. Mail order had existed in Europe since the 1500s when book catalogs were first printed in Venice. Seed catalogs followed in the 1600s and catalogs for luxuries such as fine Wedgewood China in the 1700s. Benjamin Franklin even sold a book catalog via mail order.

Mail order really started to come into its own in the US in the years leading up to the Civil War. Shipping and communications became easier as the railroads, telegraphs and newspapers expanded west. The United States Postal Service made sending newspapers, books and magazines cheaper. Big city newspapers, farmer publications and religious papers spread across the country. All of them were full of ads, most of which were for catalogs to be requested by mail.

These ads were generally from companies who specialized in specific products. They advertised shoes, candles, watches, clothing, hunting and fishing gear, tools, dubious home remedies, bibles and farming implements among other items necessary for a frontier existence.

Wholesale catalogs with a broader selection were used by local stores to stock their shelves. Salesmen also traveled the countryside by buggy representing the manufacturers, wholesale houses and department stores. One of those salesmen was Aaron Montgomery Ward, who worked for the wholesale division of Field, Palmer and Leiter which also ran the store that would become Marshall Field department store.

Ward had left school at 14. After a series of jobs for which he was ill suited, he began working in a shoe store. Many of his customers were farmers and he befriended and studied them, learning of their struggles and desires.

He used this experience as a salesman to understand the specific challenges farmers faced getting the goods they needed at a price they could afford.

The process of getting the goods from manufacturers, wholesalers, distributors, and department stores to the general store involved many intermediaries. Each step along the way added to the cost of the item. So by the time it reached the stores the price was often so high most farmers couldn't afford it. The stores sold on credit, which was often not paid; and to cover the losses they raised prices even more.

Many stores had de facto monopolies in their local area, leaving farmers little choice but to do business with them. The few farmers who were able to get to the city could find better goods at better prices. The other option was to buy from the manufacturers directly via mail order but that was expensive and risky.

Manufacturers and their advertisements could not always be trusted. This was a time of many technological advances and some manufacturers took advantage of rural people's sometimes limited understanding of the products. They used dramatic, flowery copywriting to promise more than their products delivered - if they were delivered at all.

Ward knew all of this and had a vision to sell the higher quality products at wholesale prices direct to farmers. He would use honest and direct copy to sell his products. He would not talk down to his customers or trick them. He would educate them on these new advances rather than take advantage of them.

To build trust he also connected with the newly formed society of farmers known as the National Grange. Travelling to local Grange meetings he would speak with the farmers, demonstrate products and present his pitch in person.

He was able to connect with the farmers on a deep level and establish personal relationships. He also provided real value to these farmers, many of whom were having to move away from their old world farming practices and adjusting to new technologies. He educated them about new tools that could increase their yield and that were more conducive to the Western landscape. Not only did Ward promise to provide goods they couldn't get anywhere else at a lower price, farmers could group orders together through the Grange to save on shipping costs. He even invited some bigger customers to Chicago to tour the Montgomery Ward headquarters.

In the early days, Montgomery Ward was a cash only operation. The customer would mail cash directly to the headquarters in Chicago or pay the local freight agent when the goods were delivered.

In 1875 Montgomery Ward instituted the first money back guarantee for a mail order company. Some big city department stores had similar guarantees for in-person purchases. But that was impractical for rural farmers as they would have to travel to the city at great cost. With an order from Montgomery Ward the customer could reject the goods at pickup or return them later through the agent at the local freight office.

Competition soon arrived in the form of Sears Roebuck and JC Penney but Montgomery Ward remained focused on serving rural people and especially farmers.

Aaron Montgomery Ward died on December 8, 1913, a very wealthy man. The company he founded had many ups and downs over the years but played an important role in both the lives of the customers and the history of the United States.

Setesfaction Guaranteed

One of Aaron Montgomery Ward's many notable advances in mail order was creating the first Satisfaction Guarantee. This was largely in response to attacks on the company's trustworthiness by the owners of general stores and their suppliers, who began a public relations campaign to sow distrust of Ward and other mail order companies. They even went so far as to go after Ward in the press. In November of 1873 the *Chicago Tribune* published a warning aimed directly at the Granges.

It called into question the claims that Aaron Ward made in the copy of his catalog. Ward did all of his own copywriting and signed his name to the catalog. That combined with the fact that he had traveled to meet people in person meant that he was known by name to his customers.

This was an effort to cast him in the same disparaging light as the snake oil salesmen who advertised in magazines and newspapers. However, Ward also did his own public relations. He managed to convince the editors of the *Chicago Tribune* of the company's legitimacy.

A month later on December 24th, the *Chicago Tribune* wrote of the legitimacy of Ward's policy that Cash on Delivery customers could reject the delivery if they weren't satisfied. They gave him a resounding endorsement and would become long time allies.

The 1875 spring/summer Montgomery Ward catalog included this guarantee: "We Guarantee All of Our Goods…if any of these are not satisfactory after due inspection we will take them back, pay all expenses and refund the money paid for them." This was soon simplified to "Satisfaction Guaranteed Or Your Money Back."

The following letters are from customers taking advantage of this guarantee, sometimes maybe taking it a little too far.

Montgomery Ward
Gentelmann.
        Last Wick I ordert Some Goods From You And I
Resived it on the 27 the Shoes and Foset are Good
But The Ratio Don't Give Setesfaction. I Tret it
on deferant Ariels But I Can't Make it Work to Sute
Me So I Made up mine Minte to Sant it Back and Have
it Exganget For Some Other Goods Wich You Find on the
Regarly Orders Blank I hatet to Sand it Back But the
way it Works itDDesent Do Me Enne Good So Please Sent
me That Goods,
                        Yours truly
                            Christ T. Bauder
        Have old bills were I Ordert it Is inside the
Page.

Gentlemen:

        I purchased a bed from you and am not satisfied,
It has broken. Will you do something about it. My
girl friend has the same kind of a bed. Hers has been
used a lot more than mine and it is still in good condition. Let me hear from you soon .
                        Yours truly
                            Ted Johnson

Gentlemen

The package of goods from St. Paul came last
Monday. The overcoat disappoints me - - it's a good
fit at the shoulders and that is all I can say for
it. My undercoat comes up $\frac{1}{2}$" higher in the neck and
around my middle it's about 5 to 6" too big (the overcoat). I am painfully thin I know but was hoping you
could fit me with that Ulster overcoat so it would
look fairly decent on me - - honestly one would think
I had just hobbled in from the cornfield after fright-
ening a band of crows half to death. I can't set the
buttons over as the pockets are in the way. Isn't
it possible to get a better fit. Sorry about this.
I hate like the devil to be senting stuff back but
by the god I look bad enought now without wig wagging
it to everyone I meet.

Guy H. Rollins

P. S. I bought a pair of pants too from you
last fall and they were too large but my wife tried
to fix them and I wore them all winter even after she
told me my rear view reminded her of the back end of
a bull without a tail. Now can you imagine how that
hurts my sensitive nature. Oh me - - - Say it's just
hell to be so thin.

G.H. R.

Dear Sirs:

Enclosed you will find and invoice for the com-
bination storm-screen door which fits like Hiram's
Sunday collar. It was so damm small it wouldn't cover
Mrs Roosevelt's mouth. I intended to purchase this
to cover a hole 28" by 6'8". I ordered a 2'7" by
6'7" because your scrumptious reversable catolog
stated that all sizes are oversize to the extent of
2" in width and $2\frac{1}{4}$" in height. A person is a fool to
believe what they read.

Therefore, Gentlemen, kindly sent the door that
will fit a hole 2'8" by 6'8". This is to be one of
those "Dorchester Doors" that makes a southern mansion
out of my paper shack technically feferred to as item
174C482. Hurry it along then, it's getting Coldern'
hell up here.

At the same time advise whether or not the wolf
can look in the storm panel without stretching.
When you sand your apologetic form letter, also
advise who the Babe is on page 2.

Yours Truly

Fred Hinz
Minto, S Dak.

Dear Friends,
      I am not satisfied with the corset. The longer
I weariit the worse shape I get. I look like a
expecting mother if I sit down and I do not want that.
I am glad if I do not have to look like that--just look
how it makes a shape without having it on. It slips
up above my belle. I want a different one or my money
back. New order 32C1552 1 corset size 37.

                              Mrs Otto Hartwig
                                Blue Grass, N. D .

Dear Montgomery Wards,
      When the family saw me open this package there was
a shout of glee - - I shall not hear the last of it for
a long time. When they saw the high board fence!! Can
you imagine a five foot two person 37 by 40 and weighing
120 pounds wearing this?
      I ordered a corselet # 32B1747 - not a bone in it
except slightly boned in the front and I get supple-
mented with this monstrosity.
      If you didn't have the garment , it would have
saved me time and postage if you had told me. Anyway
what kind of a corsetiere would send this one in place
of my order. You can forget the order now and take it
off my bill.
                         Nellie M Buck
                         Coleraine, Minn.

Dear Montgomery Ward,
      I ordered a suit of All Wool underwear and your
sent me only Part Wool. Just because you want Hoover
to get in, that's no sign you can freeze out an old
democrat.
                         Hilmer Jackson.

Dere Monkees,

Abouts 1½ years ago I did buy a Ridio From You
Andit has been working verey good up to yeaterday.
Then some thing gou woring with him. He do not give a
and thing. I did put a new fuss but that did not help
and thing how much do you charge for fixing a ridio if i
did send it in to you. Thre is only a humm in him and
not any of the tubes seam to light.

                    Martin S. Swenson
                    Route 3
                    Starbuck, Minn.

          I got the benches whitsch you sent to the Church
hear and why the gods sake you don't send me no ends
for them. I loose my pashence all over wats the use
of a lot of benches and no ends for them. How the hell
you think anyone can hang their feet down. Sure I
think you don't treat me right. I rote you days ago
and the preacher he holler like hell for the seats to
go to church but got no ends. So what the hell I going
to do with them. Send them right now. I don't see how
the hell some people do things anyways.
                    Mr. Peter Paines,
     P. S. Tonite I find the god damm ends at the
depot so excuse me.

Dhear sor

     Onle Fyou line to lat yous know the i sand after
Watch 95 cand last Monday May 10 and i dont reseft so
far so Ples aond at ounce our let me know. Ples
ancer.
                    Yours truly,
                    Mrs. John Stanek

Dear Sirs,
     I ordered a pair of shoes from you two months
ago and I haven't worn them very much. The leather has
begun to have a terrible odor. It smells like something
dead, naturally one feels embarassed to wear anything w
with that odor. I would like to have you do something
about them if you will please. Let me hear from you
soon.
                    Mrs. Edith Partsch
                    Wessington, S. Dak.

Gentlemen,
     Ordered two dresses from your sales catalog.
And your Chicago house sent me two just alike, same
pattern and same color. The dresses are O. K. but
to have 2 just the same!
     Am afraid my husband will say that is grounds for
divorce, if he see's me in the same dress for 2 or 3
years. Could you do anything about it. Would exchange
for a cheaper dress if need be.
                    Yours truly
                         Mrs. E. E. Tobey
                         Box 143
                         Fall Creek, Wis.

Dear Mr. Ward,
     I sent for a blanket in the big catalog sometime
ago. Am dissatified with it. The old man swallowed
a whog ofi one nite and nearly choked to death. It sheds
so terrible. What shall I do about it. Can't use it.

Gentlemen:

With this letter I am returning a diamond ring
I purchased from your mail order store the 17th of
march. The diamond is satisfactory in every way,
but the girl is'nt. Business letters should confine
themselves to busimess, but the business of the girl
is business here and so I speak of it. The short of
it is that I have no use for and engagement ring, when
I am not engaged-- and do not anticipate any such action
for some time. The gal and I can't make a go of it so
I am looking for other diversions.

Diversions always bring me to the Ward's catalog--
it's such a great "wish book". For a long time I have
wished that I could afford a radio-phonograph and now
the time has come. Since I do not have to plan for
a future honeymoon cottage, I can plan for a comfort-
able student's room. Such a room includes a radio-
phonograph.

Thus the whole matter boils down to the fact that
I wish to exchange my ring for a radio, The price is
nearly the same and we can keep on going with the
payments just as usual. The radio I wish to purchase
is number 462C717 as 39.95. The ring costs exactly the
same -- so even Steven.I wish and hope that you can
make this deal and that I can have a radio to fill the
long winter hours.

I am on a trip out west here not but will be back
in the cities shortly. Please send all communications
to 1913 Central Avenue, Northeast, Minneapolis, Minn.

Enclosed find the regular five dollars for the
monthly payment on my account.I am sorry this is late
but the break-up has been going on for the last two weeks
and I haven's known what to do.

G. Richard Kuch

Montgomery Ward & Co
St Paul, Minnesota
I got your catalog and need some pants
So I'll send you an order and take a
                                chance.
But the pants must be as advertized
I can not use them otherwise
I want some that sold at $3.98
Or none at all if I am too late
they must be roomy cut in full
of good fabric and all wool
I'll leave the choice of pattern to you
But I would prefer a gray or blue
and I usually like the deeper tones
Especially in the herringbones
the leg can be 36 or less
Just as the material is the best
But the waist must be a 38
Be sure you keep this item straight
I bought some trousers from you before
But now they are hanging behind the door
they are excellant for spring and fall
But for the winter they wont do at all
So please send some that are good
                                and warm
for it gets mighty cold here on the farm

PS. Be sure the buttons are sewed on well
    Or they'll come back as sure as hell

Montgomery Ward + Co

St Paul, Minnesota
I got your catalog and need some pants
So I'll send you an order and take a chance
But the pants bust me as advertized
I can not use them otherwise
I want some that sold at $3.98
Or none at all if I am too late
They must be roomy cut in full
Of good fabric and all wool
I'll leave the choice of pattern to you
But I would prefer a gray or blue
And I usually like the deeper tones
Especially in the herringbones
The leg can be 36 or less
Just so the material is the best
But the waist must be a 38
Be sure you keep this item straight
I bought some trousers from you before
But now they are hanging behind the door
They are excellent for the spring and fall
But for the winter they won't do at all
So please send some that are good and warm
For it gets mighty cold here on the farm

PS. Be sure the buttons are sewed on well
Or they'll come back as sure as hell

And They Are Factory Tested

The Satisfaction Guarantee was just one of the ways Aaron Ward tried to win and maintain the trust of his customers. He made many guarantees of the quality of the items he sold. Even as the company grew he always maintained a personal dialogue with the customers - not just promising but explaining, educating and reassuring them that they were getting a good deal on quality products.

In the 1880s many industries started to form "trusts." Competing manufacturers would make a pact to control the production and prices of goods. This led to lower costs for them but not lower prices for the consumer.

Aaron Ward actively searched out smaller manufacturers not beholden to the trusts and elevated them through the catalog. If he couldn't find a supplier, the company would build a factory to provide the goods themselves.

This practice was continued by future management teams after Aaron Ward's retirement and death. In 1915 Ward formed the Good Service Bureau to test products from outside manufacturers. If the products did not live up to the claims made by the manufacturers, they would be removed from the catalog or have their descriptions rewritten. All complaint letters about the quality of items went to the GSB. Eventually that would evolve into the complaints department.

The GSB was promoted widely and used as a tool for increasing trust with the company.

These letters are from customers calling into question the efficacy of the "experts" at Ward. Several of them however sound more like cases of user error.

Dear Sirs,

I am sending you per attached package 2 harness
snaps that I just received on last oreder on account
of an oversight in your army of inspectors, microscopic
analists, chemical experts, assayists etc. etc. These
snaps have such stiff springs in tongue as to make them
valueless in the winter time that is approaching together
with numb fingers. The general idea of having snaps is
to speed up hitching and un hitching but with these snaps
one would have to have a machine shop along to work
them. I wish in return a pair of snaps that are reason-
able to work. If you do not have them in stock send out
part of that army of expert buyers that buy up carloads
for cash and get them. These are the second ones I have
ordered that are too stiff to use and do not care about
having them around.

Mr. John Myer,
Granite Falls, Wis.

We wrote the customer, "We won't be able to take back
the phonograph because you have had it for two years.
Perhaps if you will tell us what is wrong with it, we
can help you fix it." The customer replied. "The needle
is broken."

Dear Sir
     I decided to order a single flow radiator instead
of a double flow but it doesn't work very good. Will
you please send me the extra flow.
                              Mr. Henry Turner

Dear Company,
     I ordered two rose-tinted ic buckets and I did
not get the green one. Only the one came and there
wasn't any ice in it so I am sending it back.
                              Yours truly
                              Mrs. Adolph Hanstorm

Telegram Received:
     THE FIRE WENT OUT IN MY STOVE LAST NITE STOP
LETTER FOLLOWS.

Dear Montgomery Ward,

I am returning herewith the gasoline lamp which I bought
from you a few days ago.

I am also sending you the bottom feetrail from my office
desk which was torn out by the bottom of the lamp when
the lamp exploded.

In another carton you will find my cash box which was
demolished by the same bottom of the same lamp.

I would like to send you some tea cups which were knocked
from the cabinet by the force of the explosion. There
were (3 of them)

In particular would I like to send you the top of our
ice box, which now has a beautiful dent in it about 3/4
of an inch deep. That is where the main part of the lamp
parked after it had made several trips around the posteffi
office.

I can assure you that it would do me a great deal of
good if I could only send you the ceiling beam from which
the lamp handed (or maybe it is hung). You will note
that a part of this same beam is firmly imbedded in the
top nut of the lamp. Or maybe the top nut of lamp just
wrapped itself around that particular portion of the
ceiling beam.

        I am sure you would enjoy looking at a nice slug
of ceiling insulation which has a nice jagged hole in
it about 12 inches long. That, I assure you, was also
make by the same lamp when it first started it's tour
of the premises. Iffyou do not care for the ceiling
insulation I could send you a charming piece of lino-
leum which has a fancy cut in it about three inches
long. /Same cut was made by bottom of same lamp.

AND THEY ARE FACTORY TESTED!

This all happened on the evening of November 29th.
I had just finished writing M. O. No. 12009, Roy L.
Chivers to Montgomery Ward & Company, Chicago, Ill.
My dog started barking and kept at it 'till I decided
to leave my chair and I was sealing the envelope to

to Wards as I rose. I walked to the door and threw off
the night latch. I got the door open about a third of
the way when there was a terrific explosion to the rear
and left of me. I saw only an oval of light that seemed
bright blue. It appeared to be fringed in red. I was
thrown to the floor and landed with my back against the
kerosene range and was not injured as the main force of
the explosion moved westward and toward the floor. I
only had a sensation of , as it seemed, having a suction
pump pulling on each ear drum. I thought nothing else
except that some one had shot at me with a shotgun thru
the West window of the post office. I knew that I was
very close to the ice box and that my Springfield Service Rifle was leaning against the wall between the door
and the ice box. I felt for the ice box and had to crawl
a short distance to reach it. I then felt along the
side of the ice box 'till I had located the Springfield.
I threw off the safety and slid the belt open far enough
ot make sure that there was a cartridge in the chamber.
I then pushed the door all the way open and pushed the
screen door open with the muzzle of the rifle. Then I
jumped clear over the platform step in front of the
door and landed in the yard. The night was very bright
and the first thing I saw was my dog looking at me as
tho he wanted to know what it was all about. I had
fully expected to see some one running away or to hear
another volley of gun fire. I still believed that some
one had fired thru the post office window, and I went
to the West end of the building and felt of the window
of the building and felt of the window glass to see if
they were broken.

When I had made sure that the window was not shattered
I went into the postoffice and found a match and lighted a small oil lamp. There h ad been very little gas
in the Ward Gas lamp and I had set a large Rochester
lamp on the dinette table so to have it handy when the
gas lamp burned dry,This lamp was on the floor and the
globe and the shade were shattered. I had not as yet
lighted the Rochester lamp. I then noticed that the
Ward lamp was on the floor in front of the ice box.
Then I was sure that a stray bullet (the deer season
was on and only closed at sundown this evening) from
some hunters gun who was hunting by car light, had
come thru the wall of the house and struck the lamp.
I picked the lamp up and noticed that the bottom was
gone. I was still hunting for bullet marks, The
bottom was under the office desk and small change all
over the floor. It was not until then that I thought

that the lamp had exploded. The place was nearly covered
with broken glass. Mail matter in the form of letters
and papers was scattered all about the office. The
curtains over the window back of the desk simply sparkled
with broken glass and I later shook moretthan a handful
from this typewriter. Some of the particles of glass
were stuck to the typewriter roll and some are still
sticking in the ceiling. There was no fire started by
the explosion. The lamp had only a samll amount of gas
in it when I lighted it and it had been burning about
1 3/4 hours.

From the first, the lamp worked just fine. We never
had a lamp that pleased us so much. We have a Coleman
that we paid $5.75 for and it caused trouble from the
very start and I am sure that we have never had thirty
hours service in the two years that we have used it, or
tried to use it. We have bought $3.90 worth of gener-
ators and pumps. We have not used it now for over eight
months. The only trouble with the Ward lamp that I
noticed was that the light would dim some times and the
flame seem to go low up to the back into the mantle tubes
I tried the cleaner at first when it acted that way but th
that did not help, and as the per formance only lasted
about 4 seconds, I simply did not try to stop it. It
would just nearly go out and then of its own accord, w
would burn right up bright again.

That is about all I can tell you. You can see what it
did to some of my furniture, and to the cash box.

Our gas was bought at Hedlunds LX station in Grantsburg
the only place in Grantsburg where lighting gas can be
bought, and that is where every one buys their lighting
gas.

I am not going to tell you what I think you should do
about it. The only consolation that I have is that
I still owe you between twenty-five and thirty dollars,
and I am very sure that I am not able to stand all the
expense of this little blow out. And let me say that
if I had been sitting in the chair the bottom of the
lamp would have hit me in the back of the head.

R. W. Portwood
Randall, Wis.

Do You Know Country People?

From the beginning Aaron Ward was focused on serving farmers and other rural people. He understood them in ways that the owners of big city department stores and urban manufacturers didn't.

His primary vision for the Montgomery Ward catalog was to bring the options and prices of said department stores to rural people. He started the company in the wake of post-Civil War westward expansion. The railroads were selling land cheap to farmers from back East and Europe. Many of the agricultural practices these farmers had used in the past were becoming obsolete. New advances in technology were being made constantly. Aaron Ward not only sold farmers the products but also sold them on the technology.

This philosophy continued after Aaron Ward's time in charge. By the 1910's the buyers for Montgomery Ward were required to travel throughout rural America in order to observe customers in their natural habitat. They even visited preferred customers in their homes and discussed their struggles and desires.

However, around the time these letters were written the management at Ward decided that there was no longer a significant difference between rural and city customers. The women in the country wanted the same fashions as the women in the city. They still sold the products that rural people needed but made drastic changes to their catalogs. The focus was now on color photographs of fashion models, radios and guitars. These changes did not sit well with some of their core clientele. Not so much the fashion choices but the catalogs themselves. They did, after all, serve more than one purpose for many rural people.

These letters reflect the challenges of serving rural customers while adjusting to modern times.

Dear Sir

I have tried every way I know of to make the horse collar you sent me work on my Model T Ford but it dont seem to fit right. Am returning it at your expense and will you kindly send me the carburator at the same price, which is, after all, what I ordered in the first place.

Sincerely,
Mr. M. P. McIntyre
Great Falls, Mont.

What is the matter with Mont. Ward anyway? I ordered a 32 V. electric churn and what do I get -- a lawn mower. Now what aan a fellow with a lot of cream do with a lawn mower?

I was in the retail store main floor, Tuesday at about 10:15 A. M. and at the men's counter, a girl in men's shorts, socks and garters waited on me.

Dear Sirs,

On August 24th, this year, I ordered a pair of
pants from your company. For almost 2 months I have
looked forward to the receipt of this item with eager
anticipation. In fact, my eagerness has caused my
postman to publicly snob me. This and the fact that
public appearence in a pair of worn shorts is uncomfort-
able and embarrassing is the cause of my unseeming im-
patience.

I have alway been a boaster for Mont. Ward. In
fact, your general catalog is an indispensable item
in our household. It is impossible to raise corn out
here, cue to the short summer season and plumbinb out
here on the frontier of civilization is still sneered
at by we hardy pioneers. So you can undoubtedly understand the pleasure we receive from your catalog, dis-
counting, of course, the slick pages.

But I am forgetting my pants which is something
neither you now I can afford to do in view of the
rapidly approaching winter. Do you think you can get
them to me real soon so I can cover my nakedness and
assume my old authority as the one who wears the pants.
Confidently my wife is becoming unbearable.

Sincerely yours,
L. H. Baker
618 Rollins
Missoula, Mont.

Dear Montgomery Ward,

I also received in this shipment a carton of 24
tissue rolls -- which we had not ordered. We use cobs
and catalogs.

Dea Mr Mont

Please cancel my order for toilet paper. Time wont
permit me to wait for it.

DearsSirs:

     May I make a complaint? And may I also say I am
speaking for 89,734,612 Red Blooded Americans.
     This thing has been on my minddfor years, but
because I am a very tolerant man, I have been able to
hold this thing back until this minute.
     Here is the scratchy problem--it seems that the
paper in your general catalog is gettint harder, stiffer
glossier, more polished and less absorbent in every
issue that you put out. Why is this? Are you trying
to make the American people grouchier from year to year?
     If you only knew to what use 99.44%(101% in the
country)of your catalogs are put to after their intended
usefulness has been achieved, you wouldn't blame me for
finding fault.
     Did it ever occur to you that you might be able
to avert a major civil or even an international was,
by working on a more tissue-like paper in your catalogs?
m   Why can't your catalogs serve two useful and pleasan
ant purposes? Do you know that you would get many more
orders if people (especially the country people) didn't
have to work themselves into a rage about once every
day? Do you think a grouchy man will order as much
from you as he would, if you weren't so cruel?

     We will not insist that you impregnate your
catalog paper with vitaminsA B C D E and R, but we
would be a country of happier people, if you would
go back to more tissue-like paper again.
     Oh, you say there arecommercial products for just s
such needs,--but do you know country people???

                    Yours foraa softer paper,

                         A A W - Pres.
                         Society for the Prevention
                            of Cruelty to Men.

Gentlemen:

Just received your catalogue number 131 and after
trying to look thru it to make an order I threw the
darn thing away and found the Sears Roebuck catalog to
make our an order without getting dizzy.

I have spent hundreds of dollars witheyou and have
always given Montgomery Ward preference on mail orders
but they must have employed some new deal brain trusters
to assemble their new catalog. You should have a round
table that will revolve so that a person can spin it
around every time you go from the pink panty section to
the toilet section of your catalogue etcetera.

If you have one of the good old common sense catalogues
and I can buy one, send it to me C. O. D. I'll nail
the one you sent me recently up against the barn and
use it for a back stop for a target.

                              Yours Truly,

                                F. H. Jahnke
                                  Alfred, N. Dak.

Don't think your new catalog any improvement. I feel
like the Swede woman whose husband told her of the
baby incubator he saw at the World's Fair and she made
answer, Tank I like the old way best.

Why Don't You Open a New Department

Montgomery Ward always emphasized the size and variety of their offerings. They may have started as a brochure selling farming implements and fabrics but as they grew so did their selection.

Aaron Ward wanted to bring the department store to rural people. As stores like Marshall Field & Co expanded, so did Ward's catalog.

The company would go on to sell cars, tires, houses, high fashion, groceries, books, sewing machines, insurance and many luxuries.

The heads of each department were required to be familiar with the products they sold and became household names through the copy of the catalog.

Some departments fared better than others. For instance both Ward and their closest competitor Sears Roebuck would find themselves foreclosing on houses they sold. Fashion was also a challenge. Sometimes the idea that rural people wanted city clothes was more sound in theory than in practice.

However there were some things that even Ward didn't sell and services they did not provide. That didn't stop people from asking. These letters include some special requests for unusual items and sizes, and services outside of the conventional mail order purview.

Dear Company,

    I imagine this letter will make whoever reads it laugh as the very idea of such a thing made me laugh too. I wouldn't believe it but to settle the augument between my husband and me, I said I'd write to find out.

    We bought a cow and she has a stub of a tail and Mr Akron has been trying to convince me and the neighbors that a few years ago you used to carry a cow tail in stock for just such cows which he says was made with some kind of a clamp to clamp on to the stub of the cow. The neighbors and I want to know - - Did you ever sell any or do you still have sparetails for cows? If so, what are they priced at? Mr Akron wants to buy one so the cow can have protection against flies. Another convenience in such a tail would be to unclamp it while the cow gets milked and thereby avoiding being slapped across the face as we milk her. We are awaiting an answer.

                Sincerely,
                  Mrs Eric Akron.

Dear Sir

    I have been trying to get a combinet or slop jar that is extra wide at the top as I swelled quite a bit and cannot get both parts in a common slop jar at the same time. I wonder if any of yours are larger. Please let me know how large the tops are,

                Mrs. H. S. Smithe
                  Deer River, Wis.

Dear Montgomery Ward,

When my baby was born the doctor did not have a a
scale on which to weigh it. The first time I went to
town I went in the drug store and weighed the baby on
the scale there.

Now my baby had all Montgomery Ward clothes on so
I looked the shipping weights of each article in the
catalog and took it from the ten pounds the baby weighed.
This made 5#, but I think baby weighs more so I thought
I would write you.

How much do you think the baby weighs. Please let
me know.

Yours truly,
Mrs. John Cross

Do you have pajamas for tall men. I know you have
other clothing to fit those of us who are six feet in
the air but do not find extra length pajamas in catalog.
Perhaps your answer will be the same as made by a clerk
to a friend of mine who went into the store and said,
"I would like to see some pajamas to fit me." The clerk
looked up at his six feet and said, "So would I."

Dear Sirs,
     Mother and I have decided that the man in the
overcoat on page 257 (the brown coat at the top of
the page) would make me a good husband. I know he
would be good to me.
     How can I get him? If you can send him to me,
I will be glad to pay the postage.
                         Yours truly,
                         Miss Martha Medford.

Dear Montgomer Ward and Company
     I must drope you a few lines to let you know that
I am looking for a housekeeper, a girl or a wife to
married. I must get married. Please send me that Lady
and dress that you wrote to me about. Please be so kind
and send her name to please let me know i 2 or 3 days.
                         Frank Vincent Mlejnek
                         R 2 B 103
                         Rice Lake, Wis.
P. S. So please let me know in 2 or 3 days. I will
be looking for a letter from a wife. I must get married.
I can not be without a wife.

     I have been told that you have been successful
in finding a good wife for a few men. I am 28 and
still single. I am of English Descent and want a
girl of my own people between 20 and 30 who can cook
and does not drink. I do not drink myself. My past
record is clear - - Ex-soldier Honorable discharge
C. C. C. Camp. I have a job now I wish to hold for
a while. I have bought goods from you before and have
always been satisfied. If possible to do so I hope
you can find a woman for me. Enclosed stamp is for
your answer.
                         Rodney Hartman

Dear Mr. Montgomery,
     I have written you before this time about where
you can furnish me various articles that you didn't
have listed in your catalog so I am doing so again
only thing this might be a little out of your line
of business but you always told me you could furnish
me with anything thing I asked for. I was wondering
if you could furnish me with the below stated articles.
     One girl friend between the age of 20 and 30
about 5!5" or some whers near that tall, dark brown
hair, either blue or brown eyes, a good common homelov-
ing girl with sweet temper and one that loves to go
to shows and dances and all kind of enjoyment and
loves a home and children better than running around
all the time - one that is not a spend thrift but can
helf a fellow save and make a good home and get ahead
in life. Don't have to be a real beautiful girl but
one that is easy to get along with and ould meet a
fellow halfway.
     Don't have to be a high school graduate but one
that would be a good intelligent helpmate. I would
consider such a girl of this kind a real friend of
mine and would consider getting married after we got
aquainted if we suit each other. Also would like her
to be of protestant faith and a real good cook and
 homemaker. Hoping to hear from you in the near future
 I remain
                              James W. Ruggen

P. S.
     Am enclosing a description of myself for your
convenience..
Below is a description of myself:
     I am an ambitious, intelligent young man, 31
years old. Am 6' tall and weigh about 210#. Have
light brown hair, blue eyes and a real good sweet
nature. Easy to get along with and am a real good
worker and am not a spendthrift and save a considable
amount of my money when I have a good job. Was born
and raised on a farm and have lived there most of my
life. Have worked at the mechanical trade for the
last ten years but would rather have an out in the
open job as inside work does not agree any too well
with my health. Altho I have a real good health now
and always have had. I have a common school or 8th
grade education and am capable of handling jobs that
require further education then that as I have worked
myself up beyond this grade outside of a school.
     I do not own a permanent home yet as I make my
home wherever I work. I own my own car which is a
Chev. Coupe and have $500,00 in cash money saved up
at present besides I have a 1,000 life insurance
policy. Would consider getting married if I could
meet the right girl.

Dear Montgomery Ward,

Your catalog has been received. You seem to have found an expert to write the salesmanship reviews of each article namely: roses, fruit trees, youngs chickens pink-nosed rabbits. However there is one thing which you do not mention - seem to have never thought of. You seem to do all else. Why not open a new department.

I'm looking for a woman. The Woman. You of all associations should be able to find her and introduce her. You have rabbits for sale. I am ordering from you today.

But dear Montgomery Ward. What the hell does a real dirt farmer want to build a new home for and stock it with fur bearing rabbits and plant orange trees, chestnut trees, pecans ,persimmons, walnuts and cherries and live all alone and lonely. I ask you.

To be plain, a beautiful, sweet and charming and lovable blond woman is a necessity in partnership on Camp Verde Ranch. Should be not over forty years of age, auburn hair, brown or green gray eyes, large mouth, small hands and feet, 100# educated refined and musical. Should resemble her paternal ancestors; her mother should also be like her father. An understandable mind and a sunshiny disposition. Should have a sufficient amount of money to become fully a business partner. Prefer a widow by law or a widow by death. What I have in mind is a certain type of women with whom a farmer whose wife is now dead two years might fall head over heels in love and endeavor to induce her to enter matrimonial relation. But why tell you this. You have no such department in your store.

Anyhow you might tell her this ranch is paid for and all mine, this is in Placer County in the foothills of the Sierra Nevadas and the New Irrigation District ditch flows through "our" back yard and crosses my back porch. There is a 10 foot water fall at my back door that sings me to sleep at nite and awakens me in the morning. A man and his wife live on the ranch with me and they do the heavy work. Oh yes, I work also and am not so bad to get along with. Have two married boys in L. A., a daughter is at U. C. L. A. and a son 18 in Auburn High School, a senior. Oh yes, the damsel should be 5 feet 5 inches tall and capable of falling in love.

It is my wish to begin with only a few rabbits and increase to our full capacity and make a real business of it. But the first consideration is a

suitable companionable woman who is fond of straw
berries, sugar and cream and who loves the flowers
you are shipping today.

Yes I am 60 years old have blue eyes, Tennessean
have a family clan down in Dixie Land composed of 400
members, all honarable but none of them will be living
with us. tee hee. Am 6' 160# bank cashier for 40
years. Most of my property was lost in the depression
but did not lose courage. Should you introduce some-
one who is not satisfied, she will be entirely free
to return to her present home in as good condition as
when she came, If when she takes a look, she does not
desire a wedding, she shall have her own way. I'm
selecting a partner for life, it behooves us to be
careful and watch our step. I'm sure Wards would not
send just anybody to enter such a close relation of
fidelity. Awaiting your pleasure, I am

Cordially yours
G. P. McCorkle
The Camp Verde Ranch
Lincoln, Calif.

                                        Saint Paul Park, Minn.
                                        Feb. 2, 1939
Dear Montgomery Ward

I am so happy. I'm going to be married in two weeks
and I am so happy and busy, so will you please send me
the following order immediately if possible:
                ½ Doz dish towels
                1 scrub brush
                1 wash board
                1 wash boiler
                ½ doz pint Mason jars with covers and rubbers
                1 doz P. G. laundry soap
                2 glasses apple jelly
                2 pounds delishus chocolate candy (best)
                2 pounds expensive nuts (not peanuts)
                1 broom
                2 mops (1 for living room; 1 for kitchen)
                1package safety pins
                Cheesecloth - - to use for dust rags.
                Please send me as much as you think I need.
I don't know much about housekeeping so if there is
anything else you think I mite need, please sent that
too. You don't sent things to Prince Edward Island,
Canada do you? If you do, plese send it to my husband
their. His name is Mr. William Douglas, Fort Henry,
Prince Edward Island, Canada. If you won't pay the
postage that far, plese let me know how much it costs
and when I get their, my husband will pay for that too.

He is a very nice man, so will be very glad to pay
for these things when they come. He has plenty of
money too, so he will be glad if you send them C. O.
D. He is smart too, and he also thinks I'm beautiful.
                        Yours very truly,
                        ~~Helen Keith~~

P. S. I think I ought to have a cook book too, and a
can opener and oranges and bacon and eggs, for the
(First breakfast the first A. M.) and egg beater and
a cream whipper too (he likes whiped cream) I sposed
I can get cream their.
P. S. Don't be afraid you won't get your money cuz
you will; he's a fur man their raises silver foxes
and he's going to give me a fur coat too.
P. S. If their's a lot more things I need, plese let
me know rite away won't you?

42

P. S. Plese send several cans of beans, peas carotts,
and beets, spinach would be good for the diet too.
Whatever else we need we will pay for too. Thank
you so much for your trouble. I am so happy.

Goodrich, N. Dak.

Not Animal Hygiene

Ward received all kinds of letters about all kinds of topics. Some were more controversial than others.

Because Ward was one of their few connections to civilization, customers would reach out to the company for reasons that went beyond retail.

The following letters deal with more serious issues than broken radios and ill-fitting pants. They seemed important to include as a matter of historical import. Be advised that they deal with sensitive adult topics and might not be for everyone.

Dear sir,

Our hygiene class is conducting a W C T U exhibit
and I would like to know if you employ people who use
alcohlic drinks. If so does it affect the quality or
the quantity of their work. Also what affect does
tobacco have on their work. Please let me know.

Dear Wards,

Can you send me some medicine so you can get
rid of it if you are in a family way. I am in a family
way and I would like to get rid of it. Because I am
not spost to have any children. So I want to get rid
of it. So please send me some medicine so I can get
rid of it. But I want it guaranteed not to poisen me
and sure that I get rid of it. It is about two months
I want medicine guaranteed to help and not to spoil my
blood so please send it C. O. D.. I pay it but I want
it to help. I will order everything from you and I'll
help you get more customers. Send it as soon as poss4
ible. Send me an instruction along.

     Yours truly

      Mound City, S. D.

Send as soon as possible

Dear Sirs,

Looking thru our catalog I came across literature
on sex and birth control. I do not know what your
books on sex are like but I hope they have the same
viewpoint that our creator taught us to have, that
is purity and not animal hygiene.

Birth Control was forbidden by God himself by
his Commandments, when he said, "Thou shalt not kill."
What mere man dares to break that law and say he has
a peaceful conscience. If God didn't intend people
to have children he wouldn't send them any. The only
difference there is between control and actual birth
of and maturity of the child is you learn to love one
and murder the others.

Another topic is your display of hosiery and
other women's apparel. Why not put displays in a
more modest position instead of such suggestive kinds.

I am sure your catalog will have the support of
all good Christian people if the above suggestions
are practiced. No business ever lived or will prosper
for any length of time by breaking God's teachings.

Whan Some Fools Pay Me

Montgomery Ward began as a cash-only business. That meant sending cash in the mail. They quickly added Cash on Delivery options that evolved over time. They were the first to institute an option for paying COD upon inspection at the freight office. Sears Roebuck would later take the COD concept and run it into the ground, nearly going bankrupt in the process. Ward maintained limitations on their COD offerings and eventually did away with them altogether.

When Aaron Ward was still traveling the countryside by buggy he observed firsthand the problems that could arise from unregulated credit. He wanted to help farmers get things at prices they could afford instead of establishing debt they wouldn't be able to pay off.

As Ward began selling larger items like houses and cars it became obvious that some credit options were necessary. At first these options were limited, but by 1917 they were offered on most items and purchases.

Customers definitely made use of them and occasionally abused them. These letters deal with payment plans, late payments and some creative accounting.

Gentlemen,

I got your letter about what I owe you. Now be
pachent. I aint forget you. Pleez wait. Whan some
fools pay me I pay you. If this was judgement day and
you was no more prepared to meet your master as I am
to meet your account, you sure would have to go to to
hell. Trusting you will do this,

                    Mr. Hans Jones

Please send me my orders as I have not received them
for four years. A $10.00 order and several other orders
I have been waiting for to receive. Please send this
order enclosed too. I am sending 3.50 to pay for this
$45 order.

                    Mrs Anna McKinley
                    Route 4
                         Watertown, S. Dak.

Bernard E. Anderson passed away on September 23 for
the time being. I will conduct the business in both
names on checks.

                    Mrs. Ellen Anderson

Your letter received and contents noted. It caused a
sort of a shell-shock to me and a great deal of merri-
ment for wife. You see it was this way, the order came
to around $46.00 and I had the money all counted out
to send and everywhere I looked I noticed your invite
to try your monthly payment plan. And as I have been
a regular customer of you folks for over 40 years, I
thought that I had not treated you right to not accept
your invite at least once. Wife said no and I said yes
so we agreed to shift the difference, I would send her
part cash and I accept your invite for the other half.
Well when your letter came, I grabbed it out of the
mail first to see when the radio would arrive, and when
I read the first line something came over me, and wife
said are you sick and I said no and I tried to slip the
letter under the table-cloth but she grabbed it and when
she read the first line she just roared with laughter
and as she has been feeling badly for a month I thought
that she had gone nuts. She read, "Your order is very
much appreciated and we would like to ship it right
away but we can't open an account now. It's not that
you haven't every intention of paying for the radio,
but we don't believe it best for you to open an account
at this time." When she finally got her breath, she
said I always told you something was wrong with you but
I just couldn't explain it and you see that guy knows
it too but he can't explain it either. He says he knows
you are honest and intend to pay, but he knows something
is wrong with you but you see he didn't explain it
either.

I got so darn mad that I walked out of the house and
out to the hog house, but I got so cold that I had to
come back. There she sat grinning like a chessy-cat
and I felt like a hog that had just been stuck. I
got so darn mad that I had a notion to write Roosevelt
and see if he wouldn't put a little more income tax on y
your fellows for the way that you treated me. The first
thing I knew wife was walking aroung whistling, something
she hadn't done for weeks and I said kid you sure look
good and she said that letter was the best medicine
that I ever had. So listen Buddy everything is O. K.
Well we have been pretty good customers of you fellows
infact if I had to shed everything that I had on that
was bought from you I would be nude except for sock,
" an Xmas present." --and wife as present would have
nothing on but her glasses. I am setting in one of your
chairs, writing on your table, everything around me even
to the stove was yours. Now listen Buddy I am going to

keep on trading with you, but if wife gets sick again,
I will send another order on your invite and you ship
me back another letter along the same line.

                 Yours Respt. The cash customer

                      Billie Hall.

Dear Company
        I am ordering the Rosedale Monument. Please send
a copy of inscription and lettering for my approval.
The reason I say in the inscription, "When the Lord
wills it" is that I am the person referred to and am
not dead yet.
                      James P Cortland.

Dear Sir;
        Please find just a few lines. Maybe you can help.us.
Would you or could are you in nead of having a man at your
Motg-Ward offace here in town. he has look for work for a
long time. Now I will tell you about him he is a Christin.
had hight school acc--worked in a hardwhere is a good mix-
ure with people neat and clean not a bracker he is frendly
and honest into the little things and very good to be on
time. age 25 years he rooms and boards here it would help
me. I am afraid I will fall short this month one went to
camp Kentucky onw is going west one is going to be married
befor I get fill up again I will fall short on my payments
but will try to pay soon as can. so don't worry on my payments cause thid is something I can't help but will see to
it what lyes in my power for I want a few more new things
from your house I need a new gas stove. Mrs. Zehnos likes
your E.L.Sewing very much they are thinking about a machine
I told her to get one like mine it shore is a nice machine
Maby it would not hurt to send them a few copys of your
damascus Sewing electric.

                    yours in a hurry----

53

Appendix

The first version of this project began as a website called dearmisterward.com. That website is still active and contains additional materials including a timeline of Montgomery Ward and audio clips of the interview of my grandma.

There is one more letter and a response that I did not include in this book. I was able to identify the subject of the letter and was unable to get permission in time to print. I hope to get permission from her to include it in future editions as well as on the website.

I was unable to find any direct descendants of any of the writers of these letters based on the information left by my grandma. If you know of any that I missed please feel free to have them contact me via the website or at dearmisterward@gmail.com. I would be happy to send them a copy of the book and would love to learn more about the relatives who sent the letters.

My grandma says in the interview that another employee from Chicago whom she met also saved letters from the complaints department of the head office. If they ever somehow appear you can definitely expect a Dear Mister Ward Part II.

To the best of my knowledge most if not all of the typos and other errors were recreated from the originals. My grandma even kept a list of words which were misspelled in the letters.

Misspelled Words

Customer's Spelling	Correct Spelling
sutctchun	suction
cipers	zippers
soposto Be garented	supposed to be guaranteed
valture	voucher
wateded	waited
snack	snagged
aswer	answer
onisel	initial
booths	boots
bair	bear
sice	size
afraite	afraid
woat coal	would call
pease	piece
a itide	excited
shaping	shipping
examand	examined
cloas	close
wavened	warn
Kenzel	cancel
Lenomalen	Linoleum
perfushnial	professional
xcench	exchange
mestic	mistake
materyal	material

saym   same
haveyent   heaviest
sience   since
Sint Lous Mosury   St Louis Missouri
narse   narrow
helles   heels
defranzt   difference
satiasfde   satisfied
dought   don't
terable   terrible
jack   check
prelate   credit
liking   teething
appreachate   appreciate
relesed   released
o hours   hours
lurn good eater   darn good either
wreal   real
dossen   doesn't
reducten   reduction
wafel iren   waffle iron
reputtlay   repeatedly
feloe   fellow

About The Author

Evan Gregg was born and raised in Amherst Massachusetts to a Sears and JCPenney family. He has dealt with many complaints from customers while working at 4 convenience stores, 3 landfills, 2 retail stores and from countless movie stars while working in the Locations Department of a dozen or so feature films.

He is a renowned complainer in his own right and likes the old ways best.

He wishes he had been able to spend more time fishing, playing Rumikub and getting beaten at tennis by his grandma.

Verna Gregg's High School Senior Photo

About The Author's Grandma

Verna Gregg was born Verna Sylvia Stolpe in St Paul, Minnesota, in 1914. Her parents had immigrated to America around the turn of the century from the Jönköping region of Sweden.

She graduated from Johnson High School in 1932 and soon began working for Montgomery Ward. She remained there until her first son Harrison Lewis Gregg was born in 1941. She returned briefly in 1942 while her husband Lewis Gregg was away during World War II.

Between her stints at Montgomery Ward Verna worked in the Gregg Department Store in St Paul which was run by her mother in law Hilda. While doing so we can only assume she handled her fair share of complaints in person.

After the war she had two more sons and worked with Lewis in a series of midwestern banks.

She passed away in 1990 while splitting time between Welaka, Florida and Minonk, Illinois.

She was well known for her sharp sense of humor, warm heart, weird Swedish jokes, and being a great storyteller.

Acknowledgements

Most of the information about Montgomery Ward came from the book <u>The First Hundred Years Are The Toughest</u> by Cecil C. Hoge, Sr. It's an impressively researched book about the history of Montgomery Ward and their biggest rival Sears Roebuck. It's a fascinating story that touches on many different aspects of US History. I did my best to summarize a huge story and could have gone into much more detail. However this book is about the letters and the people who wrote them. So if you'd like to learn more I strongly recommend you track down a copy of Mr. Hoge's book.

This book wouldn't have been possible without the help and encouragement of many people.

First and foremost thanks to John L. Gregg for finding the letters and interviewing my Grandma about them.

To Abe Loomis for his encouragement and editing assistance.

Thanks also to those who contributed to the Kickstarter to make this book a reality: Jason Mazzarino, Michael J. Manz, Nicole Nemec, Jill Strachan & Jane Hoffman, Sarah and Shawn Nevin, Lisa Berglund, Martin and Natalie, Patrick Cahn, W.P. Fleischmann, Tristan Michela, Joseph A Paul, Carlin Polaszek, Melanie Sivley, J. Alexander D. Atkins, Angela Gervais, Jessica Hickman, Kelley Johnson, Justin Leatherby, Robert Lövgren, Alison Barber, Courtney Boatright, Sharina Brock, Jonathon K Butler, Linda Bund, Jonathan C, Nellie Cole, Sarah Condit, Kent Daulton, Tom Davidson, Charlotte Elva, Justin Gallant, Lia Gelder, Mike Giaquinto, Tiffany Gregory, Nazar H, Lavoie Henderson, Minh Hoàng, Dave Holets, Pug Horton, Robert Kienzle, Jim Kleefeld, Heidi R. Krueger, Jean Longendyke ,Susan E Lund, Alex MacClellan, Heather McLean, Naomi Morse, Brice Moss, Pierre Pasquet, Melissa Priddy, John Adrian Roybal II, Oliver S, Sarah Santillano, Matthew L. Schwartz, Mindie Simmons, Francesca R. Villegas, Claudia Vondra, Jeff Weston, Gregory Whiting, Carolyn, Michelley, DY, Fuschi